# Robots on the Loose!

Steve Cole ✳ Jonatronix

OXFORD
UNIVERSITY PRESS

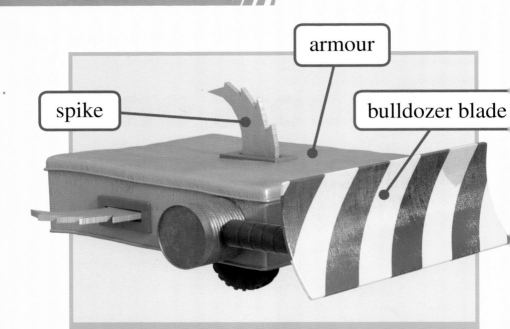

armour

spike

bulldozer blade

Robot name: Steel-Strike
Category: Heavyweight
Built by: Cat and Naveena

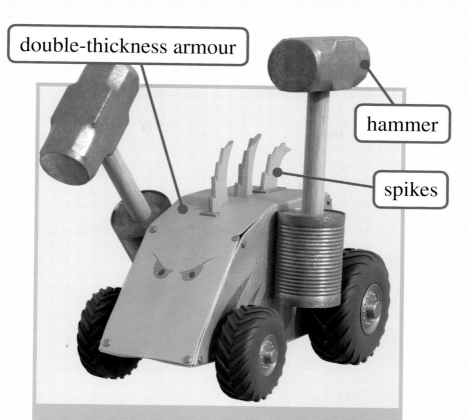

double-thickness armour

hammer

spikes

Robot name: Big-Bash
Category: Heavyweight
Built by: Ant and Tiger

# Chapter 1 – Robot Battle Challenge

Steel-Strike was a metal tin on wheels, with a bulldozer blade at the front. For the last few weeks, Cat had been helping Naveena and her dad to build the robot and now they were going to enter Steel-Strike in the Greenville Robot Battle Challenge at the Town Hall.

"I can't believe the contest is tomorrow!" said Cat.

Naveena looked nervous. "I hope Steel-Strike does OK."

"You've made it really tough," Cat told her. "Steel-Strike will make a big impression at the contest, I'm sure."

As Cat and Naveena walked to school one morning, Ant and Tiger overheard the girls talking about Steel-Strike.

"Your robot doesn't stand a chance!" Tiger laughed.

"Our robot is called Big-Bash," Ant added. "It's got reinforced steel spikes and double-thickness armour."

"You'd better bring a dustbin to the Town Hall, so you can carry Steel-Strike home!" Tiger teased. "See you at the contest!"

As Ant and Tiger left, Naveena sighed. "I bet Tiger is right. Steel-Strike doesn't stand a chance."

Cat shook her head. "Don't listen to him. He's only showing off."

After school, Cat and Naveena tested Steel-Strike to make sure it was ready for the contest. They drove it up ramps and into walls. They steered it past obstacles. They tested its bulldozer blade. They dropped things on it.

"That's one tough robot," Cat smiled. "Ant and Tiger's Big-Bash won't know what's hit it!"

# Chapter 2 – Disaster!

Next morning, Naveena and her mum took Steel-Strike to the contest at the Town Hall. When Cat got there, she found Naveena looking very upset.

Cat was worried. Had something gone wrong?

"Steel-Strike's broken!" Naveena told Cat. "Look! It won't steer properly."

Cat watched the robot wobble and jerk. "Maybe we ran too many tests last night," she groaned. "Quick, let me have a look."

"There's no time," said Naveena. "We've only got fifteen minutes before we have to face Big-Bash!"

Tiger came up to them. "Bad luck that you're up against Big-Bash in the first round," he said. "We'll knock you right out of the contest."

"In your dreams," said Cat.

Tiger watched Steel-Strike wobble and whirr. "Well, if that's all your robot can do," he said, "I don't fancy your chances."

As Tiger went to rejoin Ant, Cat saw Max across the hall.

"Am I in time for the first round?" Max asked.

"Yes, but we'll have to pull out," said Naveena sadly. "Steel-Strike's steering has gone wrong."

"Oh, no!" said Max. "Steel-Strike looks great. It deserves to do well."

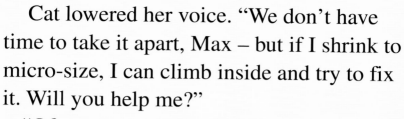

Cat lowered her voice. "We don't have time to take it apart, Max – but if I shrink to micro-size, I can climb inside and try to fix it. Will you help me?"

"Of course I will," said Max.

Cat picked up Steel-Strike. "Wait for us here, Naveena," said Cat. "Max and I think we can fix it …"

"But …?" spluttered Naveena. But Max and Cat had already rushed off.

Max and Cat took Steel-Strike to a quiet corner. Cat unscrewed one of the spikes from the robot's side so she and Max could get inside. Then they turned the dials on their watches and …

The two friends crawled inside Steel-Strike. They could see all the wires and batteries that made the robot work.

"It looks as if that piece of metal has jammed against that wheel," Max said. "Let's shift it."

Working together, Max and Cat tugged and pulled at the piece of metal. They managed to bend it back from the wheel but couldn't remove it completely.

Then they heard Naveena's voice. She must have followed them. "Er, Cat? Max? I thought you might need the remote control." She paused. "That's funny. Where are they?"

Suddenly, Steel-Strike lurched forward. Cat gasped. "Naveena is using the remote control!"

"Wow! Max and Cat must have fixed the steering already!" Naveena said happily. She pushed down the lever on the remote control and sent Steel-Strike skidding backwards. A minute later, Naveena had lifted Steel-Strike up into the air. Max and Cat were jolted backwards.

"I wonder where Cat is? It's time to get ready for the contest," Naveena said to herself. She screwed the missing spike back onto Steel-Strike. Max and Cat were left in darkness.

"Oh, wonderful!" Max said. "We've fixed the robot, but now we're trapped inside!"

# Chapter 3 – Steel-Strike vs Big-Bash

Max and Cat clung on to whatever they could as Naveena carried Steel-Strike into the arena. Then *THUMP!* Steel-Strike hit the floor with a bump.

From inside Steel-Strike, Max and Cat could hear excited chatter from the arena.

Cat looked at her watch. "It's 10.30. I think the competition is about to start. We must be in the arena," she whispered to Max.

Suddenly, the Mayor's voice boomed out: "As chief judge, I declare this contest open!"

"We've got to get out of here!" said Max. He and Cat tried to unscrew one of Steel-Strike's spikes from the inside, but it wouldn't budge.

A siren sounded. Steel-Spike rocked forward. There was a round of applause as the two robots raced towards each other.

"Keep close to the side and hold on," shouted Max.

*CLANG!* A hammer fell and smashed into Steel-Strike.

"We're up against Big-Bash first," said Cat. "That was one of its hammers!"

Max and Cat held their breath and squeezed themselves tight against the wall of Steel-Strike, expecting another blow.

Steel-Strike swerved backwards and thumped hard into the barriers. The piece of metal beside the wheel broke off and jammed into the robot's motor. Sparks flew and Steel-Strike went roaring forwards, faster than ever before.

*SMASH!* Steel-Strike crashed into Big-Bash, scooping it up with its bulldozer blade. Big-Bash was flipped high into the air.

The audience cheered. "I think we might have just flipped Big-Bash!" shouted Cat over the noise.

Then they heard Naveena's voice from outside. "No, Steel-Strike! Switch off! Why won't you switch off?"

"The remote has stopped working!" yelled Max, as Steel-Strike zigzagged wildly around the arena. "The robot's out of control!"

# Chapter 4 – Robot on the loose!

*BANG!* Steel-Strike smashed through the barriers. It hurtled into the next door arena, where two other robots were battling …
but they didn't battle for long! Steel-Strike crashed into them, knocking them apart. Then it started to spin round and round, faster and faster.

"I feel sick!" groaned Max.

Steel-Strike was off again. It crashed through the barrier and out of the second arena. Then it zoomed along the corridor into another room. People yelled in alarm and jumped aside.

"We've got to stop this thing before someone gets hurt!" Max cried.

"I've got a feeling that the 'someone' could be one of us," said Cat.

Just then, Steel-Strike smashed against the wall. Chunks of plaster went flying. The jolt of the crash sent Max falling forwards …

Max and Cat held their breath.

"Do you think it's stopped now?" whispered Cat.

Max pulled himself up. "I think so. Let's get out of here while we can."

"Look! There's a hole here where Steel-Strike has smashed into the wall," said Cat. Quickly, Max and Cat slipped through the thin gap. They turned the dials on their watches and grew back to normal size – just as Naveena rushed up, followed by the Mayor, Ant and Tiger.

"I'm sorry," said the Mayor, slightly out of breath, "but as chief judge of this contest, I must disqualify your robot. It's against the rules to leave the arena."

"I understand," said Naveena quietly.

"Don't be sad," said Ant. "Steel-Strike is the most awesomely tough robot I've ever seen!"

"I agree," said Tiger. "One flip from Steel-Strike and Big-Bash was finished!"

"Perhaps we could all work together on an even better version of Steel-Strike?" Ant suggested.

"Really?" Naveena grinned. "That would be amazing, wouldn't it Cat?"

"Absolutely!" Cat grinned.

"We'll definitely win the next contest," Tiger declared. "Do you want to help, Max?"

"Of course!" Max looked at Cat and lowered his voice. "Just promise me that we'll control it from the outside next time ..."

"It's a deal!" replied Cat.